My Fair Poetry

Volume Two of
Awakening My Sleeping Poetess

by

Sandra Ann Humphreys

PublishAmerica
Baltimore

First printing

PublishAmerica has allowed this work to remain exactly as the author intended, verbatim, without editorial input.

Hardcover 978-1-4560-5938-5
Softcover 978-1-4560-5937-8
PUBLISHED BY PUBLISHAMERICA, LLLP
www.publishamerica.com
Baltimore

Printed in the United States of America

THE DENTIST
c 2010

"Come on in," said the dental hygienist,
"How's your smile today?"
Not that good I should've guessed
And thought that I should pray

You do need a root canal
Because the dentist said,
"The tooth has rotted away, "
And those words I've come to dread

Like temporary insanity
It comes and goes away
You just pray to God it's over soon
And you'll be on your way

You discover it wasn't all that bad
When he finally finds the roots
But the freezing into the open nerve
Makes you jump out of your boots

When it's all over
You thank the Lord again
Now all you have to do is pay for it
So you get out your cheques and pen

"Come back in a few months or so,"
The receptionist says to you
So you try to fake a smile
Because that's all that you can do

REMINDER
c 1996

I wonder if I just remind you
Of a failed love
I wonder if I remind you of
A weakness that helped it fail
Am I a reminder?
Or do you remind me of a failed love
I wonder if you remind me
Of a weakness that helped it fail
Are you a reminder?
Does it fit as to why
I am so uncertain
Of how I feel
And I cannot ask you
What I am scared of
Because it could be you

TO JUDGE
c 1996

God takes the time to judge
When judgment is called for
And turns our losses into something to be found
I'll be there
To let loose all those feelings
That let loose your imagination
And believe that there is a person somewhere
That examines
What they say before they say it
All the time we lose
Feeling sorry for ourselves
Can be turned into pure burning energy
That gives life to an existing soul
And takes away the pain while smiling at the future

JUST REMEMBER
c 1996

Do you know that I never found what is a pleasure to find
It was torment
But everyone finds love if they choose to love the Lord
Catch me if you can but I'm not trying to get away
From old time misery to a brand new happy day
Just remember I've got it now
Just remember
Just remember
Just remember I've got it now
God's love that captured this weary soul
From fear and pain
Lord you handed me songs of sadness
And I tried to sing harmony
Then you handed me happiness to sing away the hard time blues

WHAT WILL I FIND WHEN ALL IS SAID AND DONE

c 1996

When all is said and done
Then we'll know where love stands
What love demands
And we'll be certain that love does not end there
But needs to begin growing roots and taking form
As a friendship of a type, becoming ripe
For the strain on love is the beginning of as newer stronger love
It causes us to act
And is tested with the rising of each new sun
Therefore love grows, branching out in the directions it needs to
The same tree makes the tree anew, with every bud in the springtime
If the roots were formed from fertile soil, with the proper nutrients then all that could grow from it will be rich, and healthy
That is like Jesus growing in our hearts day to day
So be thou wise to all your beginnings for that is the same for your ends

PRETTY KITTY
c 2009

She's a pretty, pretty, pretty, pretty kitty
She's my pretty, pretty, pretty, kitty-cat
She's a pretty, pretty, pretty, pretty kitty
She's my pretty, pretty, pretty, kitty-cat

She's a pretty, pretty, orange-coloured kitty
She's my pretty, pretty orange kitty-cat
She's a pretty, pretty, orange-coloured kitty
She's my pretty, pretty, orange kitty-cat

She has pretty, pretty, eyes and nose and ears
She has pretty, pretty, eyes and nose and ears
She has pretty, pretty, eyes and nose and ears
She's my pretty, pretty, pretty kitty-cat

IF I HAD ANY TIME
c 2010

If I had any time could I spend it with you
Heal the heart, heal my soul,
If you had any time, would you spend it with me
Lost it seems—out of control
Being with you it feels so true
Any time I had I'd spend it with you
Most of all Lord, heal my heart, heal my soul
If I had any time, if you had any time
Could we spend all of our love, all of the time
Bring it all out, bring it with you
If we had any time, what would we do
Spend it with me, spend it with you
With lots of time—forever true
Heal our hearts, heal our soul
If we wanted to shine and be in control
Love you so much Lord, my heart and my soul

IF I'M TO BE WITH YOU
c 1984

Where do you go
What do you do
Without me
I'm always thinking about you
1977
You dwell in the deepest regions of my heart and soul
Is it true I ask myself
Your indifference
Or was I just there at the wrong time? The right time?
Am I wise enough not to fall in love
If it be that I must forget you
The task seems undeliverable
I shall only tolerate your absence
And dwell upon the memory of you
Please—it will not just all end
Embarking on new beginnings
Leading us there
To the place that wants us
Even though it is not known where yet
But I know dreams will come true
Even if we are not together
But I dream to be happier with you

THAT USED TO BE ME
c 2007

I saw this girl in University
Picked up by a motorcycle man
His beard was white as snow
But trying to act as young as he can

That used to be me
When I was just thirteen
A grand manipulation
The worst I'd ever seen

That used to be me
The girl he stole away
From my friends and family
Perplexing me still today

Why he started hurting me
And how he kept on knowing
Why did he pretend to care for me
As the games just kept on growing

The abuse was long and painful
Because I did not understand
To this day it hurts me
As my heart is in my hand

That used to be me
With all the lies he told
His fraudulent expectations
Haunt me as I grow old

THE LIGHT AHEAD
c 1994

Why was I so
Out of control
I thought that I
Had a lot more pull

The little girl
Inside of me
Could not divulge
Her only plea

The best thing that I could do
Was to try not to drag along
A suitcase full of memories
Of right that had gone wrong

I wondered if
I'd ever be
In charge of myself
To be set free

Each barrier wall
Preventing success
Made each attempt
Feel just worthless

But what the inner fight
Proved all about
Was unnecessary guilt
That made me doubt

I know now that
Love to me
Is a more effective healer
Than time could ever be

If I'd have seen the
Light ahead
I'd have used the true love
I found with God instead

GOD SAYS I'M SOMEONE SPECIAL
c 2006

God says I'm someone special,
But I don't know who I am
I keep wandering through this life alone
To avoid a one-night stand

Dear Mom and Dad in Heaven
Send down some love lessons to me
To help me do what I need to do
Not blind but how to see

I pray to God who loves me
But on earth where's my destination
Every day I'm on a tightrope
Doing my investigation

God says I'm someone special,
But I don't know who I am
I keep wandering through this life alone
To avoid a one-night stand

I'll keep praying to God
And reading his Holy word
I'm going to keep on going
Even when life seems so absurd

God says I am special
And I know I just have to believe
I'm a brand new creation every day
Because his love I can receive

THEY'RE JUST REGULAR PEOPLE
c 1984

They're just regular people he said to me

But you are a special regular person you see

You've been to places in your mind

To get away where no one could find

Catching up on sleep you've missed

Or dreaming of someone you've kissed

If I'm so regular don't put me up so high

And I'll give you my best regular smile or sigh

It's just about acceptance not on a pedestal

To love the Lord and people to have a life that's full

Let's just say that the love that goes round and

Will come back to you wherever you're found

THOSE WHO FALTER
c 1994

How can those who falter
Say that they are wiser
When we all fall down sometimes
And when we get up, we are sometimes injured

DISORDERS AND DIFFICULTIES
c 1994

Why must we suffer, the tragic ones

Life has equipped us with little tools to fight

Our illnesses are not too light

For the seriousness of survival will entail

Some successful days, and some that fail

Please be strong o heart of gold

Now and forever until you grow old

Death must happen, and so must birth

Each and every day gives God's meaning on earth

Help me Lord to keep my way

Especially on this fallen day

My guard is down, I'm bent and torn

Lord, just help me rise each early morn

GOD'S LOVE
c 1996/99

God's love is deep and caring too

God's love decides what you will do

God's love designs a heart that's glad

God's love keeps your heart from being sad

God's love demands and God's love fulfills

God's love is full of little thrills

God's love is rich and God's love is poor

God's love is one that you adore

God's love is up and God's love is down

God's love starts up and then goes round

God's love is special from Him it grows

God's love is more than "I suppose"

God's love to me is a friend that's rare

God's love is only what you share

Because I think God's love is good for me

I'll love the Lord who sets me free

I'M DIFFERENT SHADES OF BLUE
c 2010

I'm different shades of blue
After meeting you
Sometimes my heart beats faster
But if you could just be true
That's really what I'm after
Someone who loves me all the way
For what I do and who I am
I cannot count the shades
I cannot stop the blues
After reaching into my pocket
Even taking off my shoes
I feel the blues in different shades
And babe make no mistake
The blues because of you
Are something I don't fake

QUOTES
BY SANDY HUMPHREYS
c 2009

"A good day is only a day away!"

"Loving God & people, burns a desire in my heart to be in reality!"

ODE TO TIM
c 2009

He'd boldly state that he's a "keener" as a matter of fact

And that was just the way he'd act

He was a fighter for the environmental sciences' case

As he tried to save us all from Tim Horton's cup waste

He loved his family so much he talked about them all the time

He showed us all his family photos he prized so fine

I miss him because he was so nice to me

He was a story-teller, an artist, a poet, and scholar so free

He showed me his puppy dog drawing he'd sketched so well

These last words he spoke to me he was so proud to tell

The smartest, flamboyant "kid" in the class

He'd tell us all jokes and make us laugh

With Jesus I his heart, he's in heaven I know

Where God's heroes, brothers, husbands, and fathers all go

If traumatic memories outweigh dreams for the future where
does hope & expectations for accomplishment of goals fit in?
c 1999

RECOVERY

Recovery is sometimes just a choice
When you are well enough
With the information you have
To back it up
You've told your story
To whoever would listen & try to understand
And lend a hand
You've mastered techniques and gained skills
And people are rooting for you
You look good in people's books
You're strong enough to stand alone
And sensitive enough
To share the love you have to give
You can distinguish between right and wrong
And you can listen, you can move on, and then let go
And do not judge others
And do not let them judge you

I WANT A MAN WHO LOVES THE LORD
c 1995

I want a man who loves the Lord
Above all I could ask for

I want a man, I want a man, who loves the Lord

He should work hard, but not in vain
He should know the love he'll gain

I want a man, I want a man, who loves the Lord

Respecting his past, he can honestly say
He can put in an honest day

I want a man, I want a man, who loves the lord

I will always expect that Satan will try
To undermine God who helps us get by
Going on without a love of my life is hard
But, I want a man, I want a man, who loves the Lord

I want a man, I want a man, who loves the Lord

HEIDI
c 2008

Heidi is pretty and somewhat rare
Her way about her is done with flare
A friend in need she's a friend indeed
Talking together to plant that loving seed
Like sisters, like two girls we danced each with a different guy
Just because we wanted to give it a try
When we've been in panic, and when we've been calm
We know when to take action and when to stop alarm
Our sacrifice is family, of course this is true
We share our love of Jesus either feeling happy or when we're
feeling blue
She cries when she's not patient, but she tries to do her best
She gives her heart to everyone, when she's put to the test
She makes a delicious turkey, a special roast, or a ham
Neat as a pin, and tidy when no one else gives a dam
She's so very musical but her treasures are in God's vault
She gives me hope I return to her, and we don't look for fault
We sing happy birthday every year because we are the same age
We share our souls and talents and whatever is the rage
I'm happy she's still there, and that we're Heaven bound
Because we gave our hearts to Jesus and he'll always be around

GLORI
c 2010

Glori is sunshine
All the time
Glori is sunshine
Like this special rhyme

Glori is the warm rain
That makes the flowers bloom
She fills my heart with happy thoughts
Lighting up my tiny room

Glori is blue sky
Like a little girl's first love
I never doubt the peace
God will send her from above

Glori is a rose
Lighting up the atmosphere
Glori's still a flower child
God take away her fear

Glori is a diamond
She shines a special light
She's never been too far away
For our souls to reunite

Glori is sunshine
God taps upon her heart
He calls is there anyone there to love me?
To make a brand new start

The Decision of Salvation—the most important decision of your life, putting God first & then your husband or wife next if you believe and are born-again.

The Decision on Matrimony—the second most important decision of your life
c 1985

To the delights of the many young and/or young at heart, men and women pledge vows of protection, love, adoration, and commitment. This makes me very happy to witness, for the celebration of love in any way brings happiness that salutes peace of mind, and the love of the Lord.

A long journey it becomes for some to be blessed with a mate, to find that total bliss that comes with hard work and dedication to God.

There is also treasure relying one oneself, and learning the lessons in life with God on your own. Some lessons might be out of the ordinary, or just not experienced before.

A WEDDING
c 2010

From this day forward
We'll share our love and respect for our maker and each other
And experience many things together
Be true and faithful to one another
And keep the devil and his wishes away
We'll travel down life's highways
Picking up the pieces if they fall
Supporting each other through the love of God
In our strengths
And in our weaknesses
We'll hold hands
We'll smile
We'll overcome the frowns
The sun will shine on us and the cold and dark rainy days will pass
Joy will prevail through our love dedication and God's love wrapped around us

TODAY
c 1985

I love you still
In my heartbeat
Even though you warned me when I was twelve I
would not for long
When it is suddenly
I think of you
I remember how I thought I loved you
As a little angel girl
Too bad the façade was that you did not love me
I will go on remembering
The love I had for you
And wondering why I did
And why today as I can recognize it I will feel
strange forever more

TOUGH ON US
c 2010

You know it is tough on me
Looking for a gentle God-loving man
And I know it's tough on you
Who may have to love all over again

But somehow it is worth trying
To find that peace of mind
And somehow stop the crying
And leave the past behind

Never to be easy
Or just plain go away
But the trials we've leaned to deal with
Keep us present in today

But still my darling angel
May be just a darling man
A complex combination
Of God's all perfect plan

I do need hugs and kisses
And maybe someone in my life
To pledge the vows and live the dream
As a God-fearing gentle wife

Someday God will let us meet
And you'll treat me like a queen
And we'll go to that special place
That we have never been

ARE YOU CRYING HEARTS?
c 2010

You may only have one...
A heart that keeps on beating
Your life repeating
But you're crying hearts
For so many at one time
You'd think your tears had somewhere to go
Are you crying hearts like yours and mine?
Then leaving them out to dry
Are you crying hearts?
Buckets full of tears?
For all those years
You never had a true love
They all have passed you by
Are you crying hearts?
For the one day you'll forget
And you will let
All those tears
Cease
And no longer crying hearts
Will be your feast of Joy

FORTUNE FEW
c 1993

Don't be sad if fortune few
Just ask the Saviour what to do
When he says to do his Will
Do not do your own, to him be true

Then, as you rest still
He will guide you on your way
He'll lighten the load you accumulate
If all you do is trust in him today

The way to do evil
Is to act your way in the moment
The way to peace
Is to shyly bear the torment

It isn't wrong at all
To seek the Lord's relentless relief
The Lord is always there
To share or remove your grief

Read his word, and follow it
To please the Heavenly Father
Then practice Hope, and Faith and Love
Or else why even bother

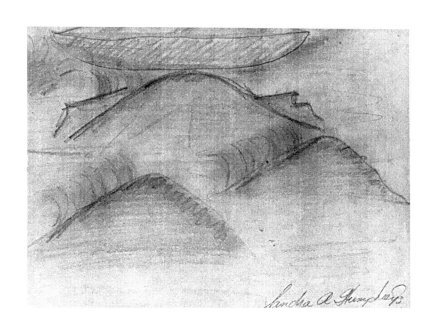

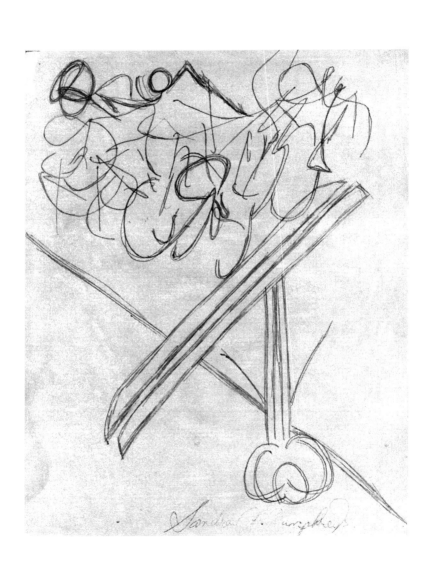

NO LOVIN'
c 1997

Can't give you no lovin'
I just want supper
Can't give you no lovin'
My day's been too long

Can't kiss your cheek
I just want supper
Can't scream out loud
That wouldn't be proper

Can't tell you my story
I just want supper
Don't have no more worries
I haven't a dollar

Won't break your heart
I just want supper
I won't treat you wrong
That's not an option

I can't go to sleep
I just want supper
Can't feel my feet
I've done too much walkin'

Can't give you no lovin'
I just want supper
Can't give you no lovin'
I just can't make the offer

I just want supper
I just want supper

RELENTLESS AIM
c 1984

Tomorrow could be relentless aim
But for today it's only time and space
I don't know it that's what's to blame
Or if I'm just caught up in the race

Days on days have passed me by
I once searched for a way of life
One that didn't make me cry
And left behind so much strife

Won't you love me for a while I cried
As I tried to leave the past behind
Just long enough to know that Jesus died
As I tried to just be kind

I only shed one tear God sent from up above
He said no longer must you be sad
I give you faith, and hope and love
Just to make you glad

I didn't ask for an eternity of love, just not to be
rejected
I asked for a friend for little a while
But God made sure I was accepted
No more to walk a lonely mile

TO HOLD YOUR HAND
c 1997

To hold your hand
Walk a million miles
To hold your hand
Give you all my smiles

To hold your hand
Along the paths of life
To hold your hand
Makes everything alright

I could drift along the "Milky Way"
By watching the stars at night
Then wake up on some sunny day
To hold your hand
To hold your hand

The others think I'm crazy
Satan says I'm lazy
God, I want to hold your hand
I want to hold your hand

I'll cross the wildest river
Bring down the mightiest foe
Die without remembrance
As long as I know

That I could hold your hand
Walk in the sand
Live life as planned
By your authority's stand

To hold your hand
To hold your hand

THANKS TO MARVIN
c 1984

I don't know why
But it's nice you make me sigh
Instead of down
You make me high

Better in a sense
With the light in your eyes
Not so tense
With my wonder whys

When I come too close
You look a fright
I'm waiting on your table
Happy to see you tonight

Months have gone by
And your poems to my delight
Set me up to feel good
As I begin to feel alright

Sometimes you push me aside
And I don't understand
But just keep on smiling pride
As I know the gentle man

TO RETURN A SMILE
c 1984

It's so nice to see someone smile
In my direction
I love to return it
With my heart's love perfection

What do I feel in you?
The person who smiled at me?
I feel some friendly connection
And as usual it is free

Reminding me of happier times
Of hello now and then
A friendly pat on the back
Shake a hand and give a grin

However it works
A smile is infectious as well
Reminds me of how I love Jesus
And how I invited him into my heart to dwell

So if you see me smiling
I hope that you can see
Through all my life's experiences
How He has rescued me

LEO & THE LIONS
c 1994

Today I went to Cambridge, Ontario
A long trip, yes, indeed
Today I visited C.A.S.H. the ceramics shop
Where Leo & the Lions breed

Old Leo and his Lioness
Were baked, & stained and ready
To be decorative, pretty, plant stands
For Raymond and his steady

A trip they hadn't bargained for
As Russ's car was failing
From Toronto back to Barrie
Our car the pack was trailing

Now I'm dropped off at Barrie's Rec Centre
I sit because I missed my bus
But I saved poor Mr. Lion and his mate
So really what's the fuss?

CAUSE MY JESUS REALLY LOVES ME
c 2003

*Cause my Jesus really loves me, there's something
special in the air*

I'm no longer as sad or blue, life's easier to bear

*He's my friend when I'm unlovable, he treats me
special too*

Without him in my life I don't know what I'd do

When I go to sleep at night, I travel in my dreams

I know somebody loves me, in spite of all it seems

*When I go anywhere by myself, I know that he's
right there*

*I'm never ever too lonely, because he's in my heart
to share*

I really love my Jesus, who always loves me back

*His kindness and support through scripture, keeps
my tender heart on track*

*I know that when I accepted him into my heart it
happened, and now I've happiness*

I prayed for him to help me, and indeed it's me the Lord did bless

Cause I have a friend that cares about me, my doubts and fears just go

It seemed like such a long time, that no love could ever grow

Cause my Jesus really loves me, my song's a better tune

I have a friend that loves me, and he'll be here real soon

ELUSIVE COFFEE FLOATIE
c 1994

You look like a fleck of something

Floating in my coffee

However minute you are, I know you are there

A piece of fluff maybe, something to get rid of

Giving me an unruly moment

So I grasp the current I'm stirring

With my teaspoon

I try to grab you

But you keep slipping away

Leaving me totally frustrated

Until I capture you

And settle down to drink my coffee

With no more coffee floaties

ORANGE JUICE
c 1996

Physical illness
Came easily to me
When I was a child
But I was never alone
To bear it all, all by myself
There was always reassurance
From friends of mine
As I lay there
With periodic flu movements
Towards the bucket
When I calmed down
They'd rush a fresh-squeezed treat to me
In a rescue effort started by mom
I thank the Lord for all of them and how they helped me
recover
And I thank the Lord for orange juice

WAS I THE FOOL?
c 2003

Was I the fool
For taking chances
I never really thought I had a choice
So I tried to learn new dances

I thought I could play the parts
With every chance I took could it be my turn?
To actually find true happiness
Without giving God very much concern

Surely if I had a choice
My options would seem clearer
I never felt I had a voice to complain
Except to turn to God in prayer

I have experienced much healing
In isolation or get caught up in the game
It is difficult to break down the walls
And deal with the guilt and shame

But I know that my decision
To keep God close in my heart
Has helped to ease much of the pain
And make every day a brand new start

TO DREW
c 1983

One day solitude can bring the most friends

Although acquaintances bound

Talent precedes worthiness

And you my friend are very talented

I say I miss your smile

And in a while

I write to you and see your smiling face

ANY AND EVERY DAY
c 1998

For so many loved on any day
God loves us all in a special way

My feelings are always running deep
God's promises are ones to keep

Dry sunshine warms us all
From the very biggest to the very small

Pray for me as I lay weeping
To dry my tears when I am sleeping

When I awake the Lord has promised me
From total bondage I'd one day be free

So I dream of all that is yet to come
And thank God whom all real love comes from

I praise you Lord Jesus, because you teach me to
forgive
And that is how my life should live

IN A VOID
c 1984

All turmoil has temporarily passed
But will my strength continue to last

I should suppose that it is not all up to me
Whether or not it is meant to be

I'm living in a void, no future, no present, no past
Yet all my days go by so fast

I'm dreaming plentifully of days gone by
They're not present realities, just tears I cry

To overcome my shyness dwells
My hollow being, just shapeless swells

Of things that where the darkness is
And loneliness exists where the past still lives

NEW YORK
c 1994

The tall, tall skyscraper density
Of the city streets in New York

The risky walks, to a store
Even in the day

The trails forbidden to walk
In the park
Leave their mark of pain behind

The bridges over water
Which are seldom seen
In the lights immaculately bright and soluble

Remaining is the apple's stem
They twist from the top of the city for the people's
consumption

But the garbage piles up beside them

And while the arts, like music, stomps, and stirs,
and rages, we draw more notes and sing more
songs

SEASHELLS
c 1994

Soft
Seashell
Listening to the sounds
Scented
Of ocean sand
Relaying
Refuge
Readily
For
A rescuer's
Rendezvous
To your
Lucky Lonely
Heart
Waiting for
Freedom
Wrapped up
In
A Foaming Tide

LEARNING
c 1994

I never thought that learning
Could
Bring me down
If my concentration
Had not been maimed
Maybe I'd be able to hear a little better
Maybe if I hadn't lost brain cells
Maybe I'd learn a little better
Quit losing and
Start winning
Lord help me find my eyes again,
And hear through deaf ears
Death to situations—I no longer want to be
involved in
Causes isolation
I've learned that failure
You have to accept
To be able to move on
As a part of life
But nothing succeeds
Like success
With my life and
My God
I'm learning that
That's all I've really got
Why experiment
These tears I cry
Aren't so much for the failures
But for the successes

I cry for the learning I've failed
And laugh for the joy I have received

THE PERFORMER
c 1984

Time is an illusion
When watching the performances of the magicians
Who disappear
Then the actors dance and prance
And strut their stuff
And smile their smiles
And say their lines
All the motions
Delighting me as I am young
Easily amused and having fun
You were an illusion of words
And actions
And anything but a blessing
But much of a curse
Now I've seen it for what it is
But even still wondering
Many places you could be
I still live that childhood fear occasionally
But it lessens every day
As I have new supports
And gain refreshment from
Those who have helped me get along
On my own
Which is not exactly on my own
Because no one can make it on their own
Everybody needs a little help and that love
That goes with it

OF YOU
c 1985

Drifting into a space
An endless trace
Of you
Remains in my thoughtful mind
But thoughtless I've become
Of you
The clock has a way
Of running out of time
We all grow old
But our time together
Will remain
As my experience
Where I fell in love
And with my heart's
Fantasy
Memory
This is all I have of you
But I will see you
In my dreams
Everlasting

THE VIOLIN OF LOVE
c 2001

I play the violin of my love
To your smile
I search for the melody
As I journey into the song of life
For the first time, I guess
But it never really happened
Before
I ache in my heart
As the loveliness of a Meadow Lark's warble
Is adjusted to my soul
I find peace in the situation
Of survival
I enjoy searching for you
In some lost cavern by the sea
Or in some foam renting a tide
I long to be embraced
By such gentleness
Which I suspect in your eyes
I risk my thoughts
Being controlled
By the beating of your heart
Standing there
As our chests pressed together beat as one

AWARENESS
c 1984

Lonely, lovely against the wind
Oh, daily witness, we all see sin
Begin for me the end of
Your stay in my space
And rent your castle's to those who'll pay
We haven't any love left for you today or soon
But we haven't given up, just what do you say to them?
I've been there and so have you
And still, at times, we wonder what to think or say
There is no answer that is plain to see
And all of love just tortures my soul
I'll be waiting for a finer view
Of all love's questions and answers
And I'll keep my faith where no darkness will fit
And praise the Lord in my new awareness

SECURITY
c 1994

You'd think some people are less valuable and others have no
flaws
Is that possible?

May your scars be transparent and your faults be too
Because if you weren't as you are you wouldn't be you

Don't dwell on insecurities, you are allowed to make a mistake
Just look to the Lord to love instead only for his sake

Remove with all your doubts, all uncertainty
Just pray to Jesus Christ, to receive your liberty

You're not a perfect human being, but you're perfected
through Jesus Christ
Then to tempt you with worldly sin, Satan won't be so enticed

If you think that you look ugly, or no one likes your wage
Just know God made you beautiful, and his authority's filled
with sage

The reason God loves you, isn't your money or how you look
He loves you when he teaches you, how to read scripture from
his book

And all throughout the Bible, God says we all have worth
But we must give our all to God, then live life down here on
earth

Next we must make the right choices, in faith, and hope, and
love
Then when we pass away from this earth, we'll live in Heaven
up above

JESUS HAS THE POWER
c 1988

My soul he cleansed
My heart is content
Never to be alone again
His love is Heaven sent

Jesus has the power
To show me how
I can have love and thankfulness
Cause He loves me so right now

My fears He calms
He gives me joy untold
He'll be there with me
As I grow old

His blood He shed
To cover my sin
He died and rose up
So I could be born-again

Would you like to see your manuscript become a book?

If you are interested in becoming a PublishAmerica author, please submit your manuscript for possible publication to us at:

acquisitions@publishamerica.com

You may also mail in your manuscript to:

**PublishAmerica
PO Box 151
Frederick, MD 21705**

www.publishamerica.com